NO! WHY 'NO' IS THE NEW 'YES'

HOW TO RECLAIM YOUR LIFE, SHINE IN THE SUN, AND BE AUTHENTICALLY YOU

CASSANDRA GAISFORD

For Ces

Who lost his beloved wife Rolin to invasive cancer...and everyday says "no" to giving up the will to live without her...
...and who said "Yes, yes, yes I'd buy that book"—because he still needs to get better to saying no.
In gratitude for sticking by us and helping my partner and I through some extraordinarily challenging times.

Thank you.

NO BULLSHIT

"You're gorgeous, you're ambitious, contrarian, fiery, dogged and determined bullshit detectives. I thank you.

We need those relentless, annoying questioners, these bullshit detectors, these modern-day Cassandras to report to us what they see, what they hear, and which way leads over the cliff, so we can swerve to avoid it…"

~ Meryl Streep

PRAISE FOR NO! WHY 'NO' IS THE NEW 'YES

"*No! Why 'No' is the New 'Yes': How to Reclaim Your Life, Shine in the Sun, and Be Authentically You* is a beautiful collection of important parts of ourselves, our lives, how we live in this world and how we live with ourselves and with each other. Each page is dedicated to one thing we often say no to that keeps us stuck or hurt or procrastinating and turns the No into a vibrant Yes. Cassandra has again proven herself as the Warrior Woman of Positive Living, Loving, and Being. She reminds us to live in our truth with love compassion and boundless energy for the joy of life."

~ Catherine Sloan, counsellor

"Saying no seems so simple on the surface. The author of this book does a great job giving well thought-out quips and tips on saying no and yes. This is a quick read with a wealth of wisdom in its simplistic form. Enjoy!"

~ 5-Star review

INTRODUCTION

Do you struggle with saying, 'No'? It's amazing how such a tiny but liberating word can sometimes be so difficult to voice.

Everything in our world is made up of positive and negative charges, which together make a whole. You have been guided to choose this book by your soul, because you are ready to question long held-beliefs and make choices in alignment with your sacred path.

By consciously affirming the holy Trinity of yes' you will move to the next level of conscious awareness.

No is a word of strength, and yes is the road to peace, purpose and prosperity.

Yes, yes, yes. Set your intention on this day and forever more.

May God bless

Cassandra

1
F*CK-OFF FOMO. HELLO JOMO

No to fragmented choices because we fear missing out.

Yes, yes, yes to JOMO—the joyful of missing out and feeling euphoric about the idea of not being involved in things of low priority.

2
SOBER SALUTATIONS

No to drinking alcohol to numb or distract.

Yes, yes, yes to joyful sobriety and mindful drinking.

3
AUTHENTICALLY NICE

No to being too nice—especially when it's not truthful.

Yes, yes, yes to saying how we truly feel.

4
FUN FINISHING

No to chasing shiny objects.

Yes, yes, yes to finishing current projects we are working on—and having fun seeing them completed.

5

EMOTIONAL UPLIFTING MEDIA

No to watching disturbing or violence saturated television and other media.

Yes, yes, yes to uplifting movies, documentaries, Gaia TV, or watching nothing at all.

6

REHABILITATED RESCUER

No to rescuing and enabling drunk or addicted people—no matter how much we love them.

Yes, yes, yes to allowing others to vibrate how they want to, wishing the best for them, and maintaining our commitment to healthy sobriety.

7
CHOOSE TO IGNORE

NO TO TOLERATING PEOPLES RUDENESS—LIKE people swearing and being aggressive.

YES, yes, yes to pushing back or ignoring—and apologising when it's us doing the swearing!

8

PLEASURABLE PERSISTENCE

No to taking 'no' for an answer when what we want to hear is 'yes.'

Yes, yes, yes to persistence, addressing any objections and pitching again.

9
CUDDLE THEM WITH KINDNESS

No to grudges and vendettas.

Yes, yes, yes to kindness, forgiveness and compassion.

10

SALUTE THE SOUL

No to experiencing inner torment and refusing to heed the call of our soul.

Yes, yes, yes to plunging into our métier, our dreams, our calling. Yes, yes, yes to freeing the daemon, following her, surrendering to her, and allowing our gifts to emerge.

11

HIGH FIVE FIVE DIMENSIONAL LIVING

No to living purely in the here and now.

Yes, yes, yes to fifth dimensional living and transcending space and time.

12

GLORIOUS GOLD

No to settling for bronze.

Yes, yes, yes to going for gold—the gold of our authentic self, our true voice, our artistic, professional and personal destiny.

13
LOVIN' THE LIGHT

No to allowing dark forces whose job it is to keep us from connecting with our soul, and to our soul from connecting with us.

Yes, yes, yes to light forces whose job it is to keep us connecting with our soul and to enable our soul to connect with us.

14

HAPPY HIGH

No two remaining tethered to the lower realms.

Yes, yes, yes to opening the channel to the higher realms, the muse, guardians and angels and liberating our soul.

15
CLASSY COLLECTIVE

No to 'I'.

Yes, yes, yes to 'we'.

16
ANSWER ADVENTURE

No to hanging onto the 'known.'

Yes, yes, yes to embracing adventure and diving into the unknown.

17
COLLABORATE

No to going it alone.

Yes, yes, yes to collaborating.

18

SOAR WITH THE SUPERCONSCIOUS

No to creating from the ego mind.

Yes, yes, yes to shifting our platform of effort from our conscious mind, to our superconscious mind—realm of the Self and the Muse.

19
STUFF THE SAFETY RUT

No to clinging to the safety net of an old career.

Yes, yes, yes to committing for a lifetime to following our calling and embracing the things that spark joy.

20
YOUR ONE THING

No to multiple job titles.

Yes, yes, yes to a single defining statement. Now when someone asks what I do, I answer without hesitation, "I'm a c0-creator."

21
SELF-BELIEF SAVIOUR

No to other-ness

Yes, yes, yes to self-motivating, self-validating, self-reinforcing, and to self-evaluating. In short, yes to Self-belief.

22
POSITIVE PRESSURE

No to complacency.

Yes, yes, yes to keeping the pressure on.

23
SPIRITUAL SUSTENANCE

No to seeking validation from others.

Yes, yes, yes to finding emotional and spiritual sustenance in the work.

24

TRUST THE VOICE WITHIN

No to eternally seeking agreement.

Yes, yes, yes to standing strong in our unique individuality and trusting our inner knowing even if everyone around us disagrees.

25

MAGICAL MUSING

No more squandering or disrespecting our gift, our voice, our talent.

Yes, yes, yes to being an artist, following our Muse, finding our voice, becoming who we really are and producing the work we were born to bring into being.

26

FLOWERING FINANCIALLY

No to overspending.

Yes, yes, yes to loving our bottom line and watering the seeds of prosperity with right spending.

27
GO FOR GROWTH

No to remaining the same.

Yes, yes, yes to continual growth.

28
TRUTH-TELLER

No to lies.

Yes, yes, yes to Truth.

29
MATTERING MANIA

No fucking about.

Yes, yes, yes to just getting on with things that matter.

30
ADIOS ALCOHOLICS

No to loving and living with an alcoholic or substance abuser.

Yes, yes, yes to a loving, stable relationship with a person who supports and empowers us.

31
CAPTIVATE

No to fading into obscurity.

Yes, yes, yes to grabbing the attention of our audience and captivating them right away.

32

ARRESTING ACHIEVEMENTS

No to hiding our achievements.

Yes, yes, yes to talking about our accomplishments because we understand that this is not boasting—letting people know who we are and what we've achieved is good for us and good for others.

It can be as simple as saying "I wrote a bestselling book that was ranked #1 in the top books on Amazon." Or, "I had the courage to quite a job that sucked and retrain to do something I love."

33

INSPIRATIONAL IMPROVEMENTS

No to complacency and settling for less.

Yes, yes, yes to striving for constant, never-ending improvement.

34
PEOPLE...PLEASE ME

No to people pleasing and and following what others feel is right.

Yes, yes, yes to pleasing ourselves and doing what we feel is right.

INSPIRED AND INSPIRING

No to low-vibrations.

Yes, yes, yes to keeping our vibration as high as possible by doing something that is inspiring.

36
KEEP BELIEVING

No to discontent.

Yes, yes, yes to focusing on the bigger dreams and passions that we wish to reconnect with even though they may seem very far away at this time.

37
PASSIONATE PERSEVERANCE

No to falling into anger or blame.

Yes, yes, yes to using our emotions to connect with what we have a passion for.

38

TRUST THE HIGHER GOOD

No to feeling victimised.

Yes, yes, yes to staying neutral and seeing every situation as an opportunity for our own change and evolution. We don't always have to see or know how and when positive change will manifest—just have faith and trust.

39

VALUABLE SELF

No to self-deprecation of our talents, passion and dreams.

Yes, yes, yes to self-valuing and self-actualisation and the evolution of our gifts, talents, passion and dreams.

40
EASY EFFORT

No to difficulty.

Yes, yes, yes to balancing effort with ease.

41
VITAL RESPONDER

No to reacting.

Yes, yes, yes to responding to that which is vital.

42
AWESOMELY AMBITIOUS

No to complacency.

Yes, yes, yes to being ambitious.

43
DONE WITH PERFECT

No to perfectionism.

Yes, yes, yes to affirming 'done is better than perfect' and seeking future excellence.

44

LOVING WITH LIMITS

No to putting too much emphasis on the emotional or material needs of another person, and thus, neglecting our own needs.

Yes, yes, yes to loving—with limits and enabling healthy relationships to flourish.

MUST MEDITATE!

No to skipping meditation.

Yes, yes, yes to meditating twice daily.

46

DARING DEBT

No to bad debt.

Yes, yes, yes to asset-rich debt.

47
EGO IS THE ENEMY

No to a tender ego.

Yes, yes, yes to resilience and courage.

48
PERFECT PRIORITIES

No to other people's suggestions.

Yes, yes, yes to honouring our own priorities.

49
HIGH VIBES

No to getting entangled in our own or other peoples negative emotions.

Yes, yes, yes to maintaining our own high vibration.

50
ONE THING

No to multi-tasking.

Yes, yes, yes to single hearted focus on the task at hand.

51

TIME TAMER

No to time frittering.

Yes, yes, yes to leveraging every spare second, minute and hour.

52

WHAT'S GOIN' RIGHT?

No to focusing on what's wrong.

Yes, yes, yes to focusing on what's right.

53

STAR-LIGHT

No to slacking off, procrastinating, or feeling overwhelmed.

Yes, yes, yes to following our star and doing what the Muse tells us.

54
EMAIL EPITHANY

No to diverting and responding to incoming email.

Yes, yes, yes to screening like a celebrity security firm.

55
GOAL CLARITY

No to unclear goals.

Yes, yes, yes to goal clarity.

WHAT IF IT WAS EASIER?

No to making it hard.

Yes, yes, yes to asking, 'What would it look like if it was easier?' and adding difficult constraints to generate ideas. ie what if I write a book without typing?

57

YES TO HELPFUL TECHNOLOGY

No to typing this manuscript.

Yes, yes, yes to time-effective dictation.

58
VALUE VELOCITY

No to being pushed down on price.

Yes, yes, yes to standing firm to value.

59
WHAT WOULD LOVE DO?

No to reacting from hate or fear.

Yes, yes, yes to asking, 'what would love do?' before responding.

YES! YES! YES TO LOVE!

No to hatred, bigotry, violence and retribution.

Yes, yes, yes to love. War, prejudice, and hatred have no place in our hearts.

61
WANTED WANTS

No to selflessness.

Yes, yes, yes to putting ourselves in a mindset of thinking about our higher self and connecting fully to what we want.

62
SORRY. NOT SORRY.

No to saying I'm sorry when it's not important or warranted.

Yes, yes, yes to apologising to someone we really care about and when it's meaningful and justified.

63
WINNING WARRIOR

No to following the path of the lost warrior.

Yes, yes, yes to being the winning warrior—engaged, present, courageous and authentic. This is real power. Yes, yes, yes to connecting fully to the magnificence that we are.

64
BEAUTIFUL BOUNDARIES

No to being unfairly criticised.

Yes, yes, yes to maintaining our boundaries.

65
ELEVATE YOUR WORTH

No to low self-worth.

Yes, yes, yes to authentically aligning ourself with our value and vision.

66
DAZZLING DISCOMFORT

No to staying in our comfort zone.

Yes, yes, yes to growth and learning new skills.

HELLO HONESTY AND HUMOR

No to struggling against our thoughts.

Yes, yes, yes to honesty and humour—which are far more inspiring and helpful than any kind of solemn moral striving for or against anything.

68
I'M 'OVER' THINKING

No to over-thinking.

Yes, yes, yes to letting thoughts dissolve back into the big sky. Yes, yes, yes to ego-lessness and unconditional friendliness.

LOT'S OF LOVING

NO TO FEELING unworthy and unlovable and assuming that others will reject us. This is especially true if we were abused, neglected, or rejected in early childhood, or suffered a significant trauma.

YES, yes, yes to being loved and loving ourselves unconditionally.

70
TA-TA TRAUMA

No to being traumatised.

Yes, yes, yes to using discernment whenever we have the choice to avoid additional trauma (such as watching films or news media about disasters and distancing ourself from drama-filled relationships).

71
SEE YA SELF-CENSORING

No to self-censoring.

Yes, yes, yes to communicating our essence and authenticity.

72

REVOLT AGAINST REACTION

No to caring or reacting about others harsh words or judgment.

Yes, yes, yes to silent or vocal affirmation of our cleverness and worth. Poisonous people do not deserve our time, attention, or energy.

73

FUTURE FIRMING

No to fearful thinking about events which are years in the future.

Yes, yes, yes to stepping into the actions that lead to a firm future.

74
YES WE CAN CAN

No, telling ourself, 'we can't do this.'

Yes, yes, yes to conscious awareness and affirming, 'I can! I can!'I can!' and "I will."

DOWN WITH DWELLING

NO TO THE PAST. Dwelling (pathologically or obsessively) negatively on what we did not do, or could have done 'better' leads us to focus on our failures.

YES, yes, yes to the present and learning to be a resilient warrior who knows failures and setbacks are valuable lessons on what not to do, be, or say, in the future.

76
CONDEMN CONTROL

No to thinking we are in control.

Yes, yes, yes to loving what shows up, accepting the reality that we have been given and freeing ourselves to let go and allow.

77

ENJOYING EYE-WATERING EMOTIONS

No to numbing, distracting, suppressing, medicating or running from unpleasant emotions.

Yes to sitting with discomfort, **allowing unpleasant feelings to arise and listening to what these emotions want to teach us.**

WHAT HAVE YOU GOT BETTER AT SAYING 'NO' TO?

I HOPE you enjoyed this book. It's short on words but big on ideas and huge on transformational punch.

BECAUSE I SAID no to typing this book I learned how to integrate the software I had onto my phone into my computer saving me masses of time and avoiding duplicating effort.

AND I HAD fun saying no to a whole bunch of other stuff too. Like saying no to skipping meditation because I was too tired or too distracted.

CATHERINE WROTE to me after reading this book, "I have enjoyed practicing saying 'No to procrastinating' and saying 'No to I'm not good enough' - although this is a very big one and will take a lot of practice."

Yes, yes, yes—changing lifetime self-defeating habits

does take practice. But it's fun too. It's fun shining in the sun and becoming authentically you.

As a result of reading this book what have you got better at saying no too?

Email me at Cassandra@cassandragaisford.com or write to me on any of my social media platforms and let me know. I'd love to hear from you. Honestly—yes, yes, yes I really, really would!

Read on for a few examples from people who said no and elevated their success. If anxiety, worry or stress is getting the better of you enjoy a free excerpt from my triple #1 bestseller Anxiety Rescue.

NO! TIM FERRIS

IN THE LAST FIVE YEARS, what have you become better at saying no to?

'Truth be told, I'm still working on getting better at saying no. But I will say this: the more clear I am about what my goals are, the more easily I can say no.

I have a notebook into which I've recorded all sorts of goals, both big and small, over the last ten or so years.

When I take the time to articulate what it is that I hope to achieve, it's simple to refer to the list and see whether saying yes to an opportunity will take me toward or away from achieving that goal.

It's when I'm fuzzy about where I'm headed that I start to say yes to things willy-nilly.

And I've been burned enough times by FOMO-based and ego-based decision-making to know that I'll always regret choosing to do something for the wrong reason."

~ **Tim Ferriss**

NO! KRISTINE KATHRYN RUSCH—
WRITING WITH CHRONIC ILLNESS

In the last five years, what have you become better at saying no to?

That little day job trick, which I figured out in my twenties, has kept me focused on my third priority really, really well. It's up to me, the writer, though. Because no one else is going to be able to keep track of what I do. I'm home much of the time. I have "free" time. I'm the logical person to call.

Until I say no a lot of times. Then some people learn to respect the boundaries. Not everyone, but most people.

That's the other thing about priorities. These are *my* priorities. They might not be yours. They certainly aren't everyone's.

I don't expect other people to have the same priorities that I do. It's up to me to prioritise my family, my health, and my writing. It's not up to the world. The world is what it is. Other people will do what they do.

I have learned to say no more than yes, to draw

boundaries around important parts of my life, and to know both my strengths and my limitations.

And that helps me with the priorities.

This is part of my book *Writing With Chronic Illness* that will appear late spring 2019.

~ Kristine Kathryn Rusch
www.kriswrites.com

FREE WORKBOOK!

The Passion Journal: The Effortless Path to Manifesting Your Love, Life, and Career Goals

Thank you for your interest in my new book.
To show my appreciation, I'm excited to be giving you another book for FREE!

Download the free *Passion Journal Workbook* here>>https://dl.bookfunnel.com/aepj97k2n1

I hope you enjoy it—it's dedicated to helping you live and work with passion, resilience and joy.

You'll also be subscribed to my newsletter and receive free giveaways, insights into my writing life, new release advance alerts and inspirational tips to help you live and work with passion, joy, and prosperity. Opt out at anytime.

EXCERPT: ANXIETY RESCUE

PRAISE FOR ANXIETY RESCUE

"Cassandra's book is for anyone interested in ending anxiety issues, but also, for those who seek deeper meaning in their lives. *Anxiety Rescue* covers a range of healing methods and a variety of topics, from self-acceptance, to prosperity. It's a book about total well-being. Cassandra restates the wisdom of Leonardo Da Vinci, Coco Chanel and other important historical and modern-day figures who have much to teach about authenticity and success. An uplifting, informative and inspirational work! I highly recommend *Anxiety Rescue*."

~ **Valeria Teles**
author of *Fit For Joy*

"Cassandra explores the nature of anxiety and the effect it has on our physical, emotional, and spiritual self. She draws on much of her research and writings from others of her self-help books. In true Cassandra Gaisford style of practical application - this book is for committed self-helpers."

~ **Catherine Sloan**
Counselor

"Lighthearted and uplifting! *Anxiety Rescue* is a book with a catalog of ideas, intertwined with the historical endeavors of Leonardo da Vinci and Coco Chanel. Learning about these two people while navigating how to rid my life of anxiety was fun and playful. I'm grateful to the author for taking this approach as I feel like I have a path that can easily be followed now. I highly recommend this book!"

~ **Chelsea Behrens**
Creator of *Leading with Authenticity*

This book is dedicated to love.
And to my muses and mentors—
Leonardo da Vinci and Coco Chanel who inspire me with
their resilience, courage and fortitude...
Lorenzo, my Templar Knight,
who encourages and supports me
to make my dreams possible...
And to all my clients
who have shared their challenges with me,
and allowed me to help make their dreams come true.
Thank you
for inspiring me.

PREFACE

"Nothing beautiful in the end comes without a measure of some pain, some frustration, some suffering."

~ His Holiness the Dalai Lama

CONTENTS

Introduction	95
About This Book	99
Author's Note	109
My Story	115
1. What Is Anxiety?	120
2. Treating Anxiety	125
3. What Makes You Anxious?	132
Did you enjoy this excerpt?	137
Also by the Author	139
Follow Your Passion to Prosperity Online Course	142
Further Resources	143
Blossom	149
About the Author	151
Stay In Touch	153

INTRODUCTION

Are you feeling anxious? Despondent? Stressed or lacking energy? Sadly, you're not alone. We live in an incredibly toxic world. Anxiety, depression, and other low-vibe feelings impact so many people's mental wellbeing.

As Lady Gaga once said, "There is a lot of shame attached to mental illness, you feel like something is wrong with you...but you can't help it when in the morning you wake up, you are so tired, you are so sad, you are so full of anxiety and the shakes that you can barely think...but (opening up about mental health) was like saying this is a part of me and that's okay."

Life can be incredibly tough—more so, if you're living life raw, not dumbing or numbing your anxiety by escaping into booze, drugs or some other seemingly helpful strategy.

As you'll discover, alcohol and other forms of self-medication only make anxiety worse. Denial and dampening down feelings only deepens wounds and worries that crave to be heard, helped, and healed.

Throughout *Anxiety Rescue* you'll find a smorgasbord of helpful, timely strategies. As you'll quickly discover, it's all about proactively embracing healing thoughts and healthy behaviors.

Whether it's your mind, body, or soul that needs a lift, you'll see that everything is connected. Even the darkness, despondency, and despair—the joy, the happiness, and radiant bliss.

Without darkness there would be no light. Without winter there would be no summer. Without bad times there would be no happy times. Without some anxiety you'd have nothing to warn you that you need to make a change, restore some balance, or heal a buried part of you.

Sometimes, it can be hard to delve deep, or find ways to bounce back from life-sucking events and toxic people. Life can knock you around. Sometimes it can feel as though setbacks come in unrelenting waves.

You can feel like you are drowning in a sea of negativity. You can lose hope. If this feels like you, *Anxiety Rescue* comes to your aid. Developing resilience will be some of many helpful tools you'll learn on the way.

We are not born with a fixed, unchangeable amount of resilience. It is a muscle that everyone can build, a skill anyone can master. Armed with new knowledge you can rebound from setbacks. You can learn how to find strength in the face of adversity. And you can build your courage muscles and fire up your determination to live a life of passion, love, and joy.

I'm passionate about helping people find happiness and joy. I know from experience, you health is truly where wealth lies. As a holistic therapist I genuinely care about your health and well-being. Happier, healthier people contribute to happier, healthier communities.

I hope this book provides some helpful insights and

strategies to help you flourish in the wake of any current and future demands you may be experiencing.

You'll find strategies that I've used successfully, personally and professionally to end anxiety, manage stress, and find strength in the face of calamity.

What would Leonardo da Vinci or Coco Chanel do?

Everyday problems solved by history's most remarkable men and women.

One of my favourite strategies is looking at the success and wellbeing strategies of people I admire. Success and happiness is living life on your terms and no one knows this better than the ultimate freedom-fighters Leonardo da Vinci and Coco Chanel.

That's why *Anxiety Rescue* offers fresh, fun—and scientifically validated—easy to follow, and simple actionable steps to help you tame anxiety, manage stress, overcome depression, change careers, improve your relationships—and more.

Before we continue, there's just one thing you need to know about this book.

ABOUT THIS BOOK

Anxiety Rescue offers a progressive program of holistic—mental, emotional, physical and spiritual—study, guiding you through essential concepts, themes, and practices on the path to well-being, joy, and happiness.

For many people, the approach is nothing less than transformational. More than a collection of thoughts for the day,

Why I wrote this book

I'm a New Zealand trained and qualified holistic therapist. Throughout my counseling and psychology studies, I was so disillusioned and disappointed by the emphasis given to disease and pathologizing those with mental 'illness'.

Frustrated and craving new solutions, I drew my inspiration from the work of leading Māori health advocate and researcher Professor Sir Mason Durie.

Durie created a health and wellness model known as to *Te Whare Tapa Whā*. *Whare*, in Māori, means home, and with its four pillars of health, Durie's model emphasizes the importance of an integrated approach to health and wellbeing.

Twenty or so years ago talk of holistic health, especially those that integrated spiritual aspects to healing, was considered akin to witchcraft, and certainly not treated seriously. I'm heartened to see conventional practitioners have caught up with what many indigenous people have long known to be true.

Thinking of health as a home is a beautiful way to come back to yourself. To come home—where your heart is. Where you feel safe.

The whare, known as Te Whare Tapa Whā, has four walls and each wall represents a different dimension of health.

These four pillars are:
- **Taha tinana (physical health)**
- **Taha wairua (spiritual health)**
- **Taha whānau (family health)**
- **Taha hinengaro (mental & Emotional health)**

With its strong foundations and four equal sides, it powerfully and simply illustrates the four dimensions of wellbeing that are core to the tools I share throughout *Anxiety Rescue*.

Should one of the four dimensions be missing, neglected, or in some way damaged, a person, or a community, may become 'unbalanced' and subsequently unwell. No doubt you've experienced this yourself—either within your own 'home' or within the larger, extended home of our communities and the world at large.

We know that 40 million people over the age of 18 suffer from anxiety disorders in the United States alone.

That statistic alone tells you something is seriously out of balance.

Interestingly, many of my anxious, stressed, or depressed clients who come to counseling or coaching session tell me that one of the things they'd most like to achieve is balance. Yet, in almost all cases they don't know what that means or looks like, or in what areas they are out of balance.

All too often, their nutrition is woeful and exercise seriously lacking (physical health). Similarly, the spiritual dimension is largely neglected or totally ignored. Thoughts and emotions, riddled with stress and anxiety, skew downwards, and relationships are under duress.

Happily, where there's a problem, there's a cure. Worryingly, some statistics suggest only 36.9% of those suffering seek treatment even though anxiety is highly treatable —naturally.

The Eight Principles of Success

Leonardo da Vinci was a systems thinker who recognized and valued the interconnectedness of everything. He can teach us many lessons, including the link between passion and inspiration, mental strength, emotional resilience, spiritual power, health, and well-being, empowering relationships, smart goals and authentic success.

I've sectioned *Anxiety Rescue* into a cluster of principles. Principles aren't constricting rules unable to be shaped, but general and fundamental truths which may be used to help guide your health, wellbeing and lifestyle choices.

Expanding upon Te Whare Tapa Whā, Anxiety Rescue takes a broader look at what it means, and what it takes, to be successful. Work-related anxiety is a major source of stress—one, along with other triggers, we will address within this book.

The quest for success, as you'll discover, can trigger many people's stress and anxiety. However, too often we think too narrowly, or not at all, about what really matters—which is why I'm placing success center stage throughout *Anxiety Res*cue.

Success includes maintaining good health, energy, and enthusiasm for life, fulfilling relationships, creative freedom, well-being, peace of mind, happiness and joy. Success also includes the ability to achieve your desires—whatever these may be.

Let's look briefly at The Eight Principles of Success and what each will cover:

Principle One, "The Call For Success" will help you explore the truth about success and define success on your own terms. You'll discover the rewards and 'realities' of success, and intensify success-building beliefs.

Principle Two, "Empower Your Success," will help you learn why igniting the fire within, love, and heeding the call for passion is the cornerstone of future success. You'll clarify who you really are and who you want to be, discover your elemental, signature strengths, and clarify your passion criteria.

Sight was the sense Leonardo and Coco valued above all else. **Principle Three, "Empower Your Vision,"** will help you clarify and visualize what you really want to achieve. You'll then be better able to decide where best to invest your time and energy. You'll also begin exploring ways to develop your life and career in light of your passions and life purpose, maintain focus and bring your vision into successful reality.

Principle Four, "Empower Your Spirit," urges you to pay attention to the things that feed your soul, awaken your curiosity, stir your imagination and create passion in your life.

Principle Five, "Empower Your Mind," looks at ways to cultivate a success mindset. You'll also identify strategies to overcome obstacles and to maximize your success, and ways to work less but achieve more to gain greater balance and fulfillment.

Your health is your wealth yet it's often a neglected part of success. **Principle Six, "Empower Your Body,"** recognizes the importance of a strong, flexible and healthy body to your mental, emotional, physical and spiritual success.

You'll be reminded of simple strategies which reinforce the importance of quality of breath, movement, nutrition, and sleep. Avoiding burnout is also a huge factor in attaining and sustaining success. When you do less and look after yourself more, you can and will achieve success.

Principle Seven, "Empower Your Relationships" will help you boost your awareness of how surrounding yourself with your vibe tribe will fast-track your success, and when it's best to go it alone.

Anxiety Rescue ends with **Principle Eight, "Empower Your Work"** emphasizes the role of authenticity and being who you are. You'll also learn how to 'fake it until you make it' and be inspired by others success. Importantly you'll learn how following your own truth will set you free.

How To Best Enjoy This Book

Think of *Anxiety Rescue* like a shot of espresso. Sometimes one quick hit is all it takes to get started. Sometimes you need a few shots to sustain your energy. Or maybe you need a bigger motivational hit and then you're on your way.

You're in control of what works best for you. Go at your own pace, but resist over-caffeinating. A little bit of guidance here-and-there can do as much to fast-track your success, as consuming all the principles in one hit.

Skim to sections that are most relevant to you, and return to familiar ground to reinforce home-truths. But most of all enjoy your experience.

Less is More

If you've recently picked up this book the chances are you're feeling anxious and perhaps overwhelmed. If you're like me, and many of my clients, less really is more when it comes to digesting information—no matter how beneficial.

For this reason, I've created *Anxiety Rescue* as a two-part book. Each book stands alone and shares the anxiety rescue strategies of Leonardo da Vinci and Coco Chanel—and many other successful artists, business people, and inspiring personalities.

As Buddha once said, "There is a most wonderful way to help living beings overcome grief and sorrow, end pain and anxiety, and realize the highest happiness. That way is the establishment of mindfulness."

Each book in the *Anxiety Rescue* series will help you mind your way to health—naturally and holistically.

This may be a little book, but the concrete steps and practical tools I share in these pages are powerful solutions regardless of your goals, profession, skills, experience, age, and current situation.

They're a seamless blend of ancient wisdom and modern science. They are timeless and limitless, so it's never "too late" or "too soon" to bounce away from anxiety and despair towards great freedom and joy.

Anxiety Rescue offers short, sound-bites of stand-alone readings designed to help you cultivate resilience and awareness amid the challenges of daily living.

More than a collection of thoughts for the day, *Anxiety Rescue* offers a progressive program of holistic—mental, emotional, physical and spiritual—study, guiding you through essential concepts, themes, and practices on the path to well-being, joy, and happiness.

The teachings are gently humorous, sometimes challenging, occasionally provocative, but always compassionate and kind, and, I hope, seemingly infinitely wise—and easy to apply

All that I share are strategies that have worked for me personally through many of my own life challenges, and for my clients in my professional work as a holistic therapist, counselor, and empowerment coach.

Anxiety Rescue features the most essential and stirring passages from my previous books, exploring topics such as: meditation, mindfulness, positive health behaviors, and working with fear, depression, anxiety, and other painful emotions. *Anxiety Rescue* expands upon my previous books in that it encourages a more playful approach to the seriousness of life and the ever-present stressors we all face.

Through the course of this book, you will learn practical, creative and simple methods for heightening awareness and overcoming habitual patterns that block happiness and joy and hold you back.

My hope is that next time you are faced with a setback or adversity, one simple phrase will come to mind: "Love what arises." And then, having been reminded that bouncing back from setbacks in an accepting and loving manner is the test of your power, that you will then go quickly into resilience mode and apply the strategies you have learned in this book.

If when next faced with a challenge, your default thoughts are 'allow', and 'how can I love what shows up?' then I will consider this book a success.

How to Use This Book

There is no 'right' or 'wrong' way to work with *Anxiety Rescue*. It's a very flexible tool—the only requirement is that you use it in a way that meets your needs. For example, you may wish to work through the book and exercises sequentially. Alternatively, you may wish to work intuitively and complete the exercises in an ad hoc fashion. Or just start where you need to start.

Each chapter can be read independently. You may wish to read a chapter each week, fortnight or month. Or you may wish to use your intuition and select a page at random, or simply follow your curiosity.

Web links throughout the book and the supplementary resources will help encourage further moments of insight, inspiration, and clarity about the anxiety cure that's right for you.

Extra Support: Anxiety Rescue Companion Workbook

Anxiety Rescue (the book) offers you information about overcoming anxiety, building resilience and finding joy. Reading a book is great but applying the teachings and writing things down in a dedicated space helps bring the learning alive, deepens your self-awareness, and enables you to make real-world change. Reading gives you knowledge, but reflecting upon and applying that knowledge creates true empowerment.

By writing and recording your responses you're rewriting the story of your life. As Seth Godin states, "Here's the thing: The book that will most change your life is the book you write. The act of writing things down, of justifying your actions, of being cogent and clear, and forthright—that's how you change."

The Anxiety Rescue Companion Workbook will support you through the learning and show you how to create real and meaningful change in your life...simply and joyfully.

So... are you ready? Are you ready to dramatically improve your happiness, success and personal fulfillment? If you've come this far, I think you are...

Let's get going...

AUTHOR'S NOTE

It always really touches me when I realize that what I do has an impact on people. We've all been through tough situations. Not many of us escape childhood unscathed. Few of us survive working life or relationships without scars. I work from that experience. If what I say, write, or do inspires people or gives them strength, courage, or hope, I'm over the moon.

Like many of my books, I write to inspire myself. I take issues I am struggling with, or new learnings that have deeply impacted me, and share them in my books.

Anxiety Rescue is one of these books. I'm tempted to say that it's a concise guide to overcoming anxiety and making the most of your life. It is. And it isn't.

As I wrote this book, so many factors which impact anxiety came to light. Many of them are ignored by general practitioners and doctors—the very people many of us go when we're feeling stressed, anxious, or just plain unwell. Some, are viewed skeptically by psychologists and psychiatrists.

Yet times are changing, the old ways aren't working.

Prescription medication and pharmaceutical drugs are being consumed in exploding quantities, and still, anxiety rates and other mental illnesses are still soaring.

Increasingly science is validating what ancient wisdom has been telling us for years. You only have to consider how main-stream meditation, yoga, acupressure, and other holistic therapies have become, to witness the emergence.

Anxiety Rescue is based on clinically-proven techniques and integrates modern science with other healing modalities.

From my own professional and personal experience, I know we can heal ourselves. A great deal many people don't need pills to feel calm, happy, healthy, and inspired. Some do.

I am not against prescription drugs, but what concerns me, as it may you, is that many anxious, stressed, and depressed people are not offered a choice. Nor do they benefit from someone taking an inventory of their life and analyzing the traumatic events or stressors that may be impacting their anxiety levels.

Like Len, who, aged 42-year-old man who had suffered work-related burnout, and sought relief from his doctor. He was, quite rightly, alarmed that his doctor told him that the only cure was medication. He left his doctor's office empty-handed.

Ten years later, a diagnosis of complex trauma, not only made sense but also provided a roadmap to lasting healing. I'll be sharing more of his story in a book I plan to write called, Leaving Jehovah—Surviving the Cult of Toxic Control and Shame.

Or, Sarah, who'd been taking anti-depressants for years but had noticed her anxiety rates returning and no longer wanted to be on medication. Counseling and engaging in talk-therapy gave a voice to wounds she had repressed. When darkness was brought to light, and armed with new tools of self-care, including meditation and nutrition, her anxiety rates disappeared.

I'm not bagging medication. Not by any means. My purpose in writing *Anxiety Rescue* is to share alternative routes to healing—lasting ones that enable you to be empowered and chose the best course of action for you.

No two people are the same. We have not had the same childhoods, the same school experiences, or workplace trauma. I speak from my own experience—both what has worked for me, and what has worked for my clients.

With over twenty-five years of expertise working in therapeutic professions, most lately as a child therapist and relationship counselor, I know what works.

As you'll read in the chapter, "My Story," I've swum through a tsunami of trauma, hurts, and humiliations and drawn on a range of modalities to help me not just survive, but also thrive.

My hope is in reading this book, you will emerge stronger, happier, healthier, and more thankful too.

A large part of my healing has involved following my joy—something you'll learn to discover for yourself in this book.

I use my passion journal to visualize, gain clarity, and create my preferred future—including my health goals. My clients find this works for them too—along with the other strategies I share in *Anxiety Rescue*.

In this era of anxiety and distraction, the need for simple, life-affirming, health-enhancing messages is even more important. If you are looking for inspiration and practical tips, in short, sweet sound bites, this guide is for you.

Similarly, if you are a grazer, or someone more methodical, this guide will also work for you. Pick a page at random, or work through the four pillars of health sequentially.

I encourage you to experiment, be open-minded and try new things. I promise you will achieve outstanding results.

Let experience be your guide, as it has been mine. Give your brain a well-needed break. Let go of 'why', and embrace how you *feel*, or how you want to feel. Honor the messages from your intuition and follow your path with heart.

Laura, who at one stage seemed rudderless career-wise, did just that. Workplace stress was a major source of her anxiety. Finding her passion and following her joy sparked a determination to start her own business. She felt the fear and went for it anyway, emboldened by a desire to live and work like those she looked up to. It was that simple.

As with all of my books, many of the examples I share were inspired by true events in my own life. At the time of writing, I recalled one of the first times I trusted the spiritual realm. I was a teenager when my paternal grandmother was channeled by a psychic and my disbelieving and skeptical self was asked, "Your grandmother says you don't believe she is here. But she is holding out a flower, and she is asking, 'Do you remember the jasmine flowers growing over the house?'"

I didn't.

But when I drove home I called into to Araby Lodge, where my grandmother used to live, and where until her death, she bred and trained her beloved horses. At the time my father lived in her house. I asked him, "What is that vine growing over the house?"

I didn't want to tell him anything about what the psychic had said because I was still skeptical and I didn't want to influence the answer. My father said, "Oh, that old jasmine vine? That's been there forever."

My heart nearly leaped out of my chest. It was at that point that I began to believe in spiritual and psychic phenomena, and in time, many years later, to awaken my own gifts. These gifts weren't awakened without considerable anxiety—something I talk more about in the chapter, "Shadow Work."

It's a timely reminder of just how far following my passion and being free to be me has taken me—the shy girl who was once afraid of being seen and was terrified of her ability to channel.

As I share in many of my books I hope the following quote is as apt for you as it was for me:

"Your staying in the shadows doesn't serve the world."

Here's to learning from our anxiety and transforming our lives with passion, joy, and purpose!

MY STORY

I'VE EXPERIENCED some horror work experiences during my life and career—everything from toxic shaming, acute bullying, and being physically threatened. As recently as last year, I experienced the ruthless, underhand, malicious tactics of a narcissistic woman who tried to destroy my career.

Unsurprisingly, all of these experience increased my anxiety levels. Had I not trained to be a therapist and invested so much time and energy in self-care and resilience strategies I'm not sure I could have coped. Many of these strategies, and those that have helped my clients, I share in the pages that follow.

For most of my childhood, and well into my adulthood, I suffered from what I now know was social anxiety. For many, many years it remained undiagnosed and untreated. Were it not for the wise counsel of a psychic who encouraged me to turn my wounds into healing by training to become a counselor, I may still be suffering silently.

The source of my anxiety can be attributed in part to narcissistic abuse and toxic shaming. Some healers have attributed it to a past-life trauma that I carried forward into this life—telling me that I walk the path of jealousy and that relationships are my greatest challenges, but also most my powerful avenues of healing.

You may not believe in past lives or reincarnation and you do not need to in order to benefit from the help contained within this book and others in the *Anxiety Rescue* series.

But, in the spirit of authenticity, it feels important to share how I have experienced much healing by journeying into the mystery of mysteries—both the body's and the soul's journey. It is for this reason, amongst others that I have devoted a whole section to spiritual health.

I learned later in life, and continue to learn, that healing this family trauma and helping others is my soul purpose in this lifetime.

My purpose can be summed up in one word—love.

To help others love and be loved in return, including self-love and valuing ourselves more than the poisons we may have ingested from people, experiences, circumstances, as we go through this lifetime.

However, it took me many years to find the gift of my anxiety. My hope is that by writing *Anxiety Rescue*, I may speed up this journey for you.

My anxiety was so bad for most of my teens I tried to drink my way to confidence and numb my anxious feelings with alcohol. In fact, for many years I was so acutely self-conscious I wore green foundation under my makeup to try to hide my blushing face.

People used to call me 'beetroot' and laugh at me. I was also mercilessly body shamed during my childhood and teenage years. Honestly, for so much of my life all I wanted to do was hide. Often I didn't care if I lived or died.

Anxiety will do that to you—until you befriend it and learn what it wants you to know.

When I was planning my wedding in my late twenties, I wanted a table down the back where no one could see me. Have you ever been to a wedding where the bride wanted to hide?

That's why untreated anxiety is so cruel. It can make us want to stay in the shadows. It can prevent us from standing in the light. Anxiety left unchallenged can deny us from acknowledging our gifts. It can also leave us splintered, in denial or fear or shame, of those aspects of our personality we need to wield from time to time but have been taught to devalue and deny.

Saying no to denying who we really are and who we truly want to be and showing up, warts and all reduces anxiety. Self-acceptance and integration of the polarities within us—the light and the dark, the fear and the courage, the sadness, and the anger, the anger and the joy, and the other dualities that, unless befriended wage war within, is the road to inner peace.

We'll dive deeper into the value of integrating shadow work in *Anxiety Rescue*.

For many years I didn't live authentically. I tried, somewhat unsuccessfully, to be someone else. I tried to be who others wanted me to be. Sometimes this was an act of self-preservation driven by fear. Often it was a mistaken belief about my value and the value of my gifts.

As I've shared in many of my other self-empowerment books, I was once told that I had the soul of an artist. Actively discouraged in childhood, for a long time I'd closed off that side of me. I began my career as a bank teller, then as an accountant, then as a recruitment consultant, followed by more 'business-minded' careers.

Each time I went further and further away from who I truly was and the things that gave me joy.

As you'll discover in *Anxiety Rescue*, reclaiming joy and living on purpose is a powerful antidote for anxiety. It offers holistic, integrated healing on so many levels—mind, body, and soul.

Recently, in my early fifties, I was been diagnosed with generalized trauma. All I can say is 'Wow! What a relief!'

No wonder life has felt such a struggle,

Generalized trauma is similar to Post Traumatic Stress Disorder, except that rather than being caused by one traumatic event, it covers a multitude of traumatic events.

Essentially, as Dr. Diane Langberg, Clinical Psychologist and Co-Leader of the Global Trauma Recovery Institute, says if you suffer generalized trauma you've effectively been marinated in trauma from an early age.

Talk about toxicity in the body.

I count myself lucky. Which may surprise you. But as you'll discover in *Anxiety Rescue,* when we befriend our anxiety we can find great fulfillment, purpose, and joy.

As the Persian poet and philosopher Rumi once said, "Our wounds are where the light comes in."

Light, love, kindness, hope—these positive energies provide the healing balm we all need.

My trauma, my anxiety, and my depression has led me to my Dharma or my purpose in life. My hope is that all that I share in *Anxiety Rescue* will help you too.

Much love to you

Cassandra

1
WHAT IS ANXIETY?

ANXIETY CAN FEEL LIKE CANCER—ALL invasive and equally as disruptive. But it's not cancer. You can't cut it out, section it, or annihilate with chemical warfare. Anxiety is a feeling. It's got plenty to say and very often a lot to teach you.

You can ignore it, befriend it, or tackle it– but you can't repress it. Not for long. Somewhere, somehow your body keeps the score. The best approach is a multifaceted one, as you will discover, in *Anxiety Rescue*.

Shame, guilt, blame, loss, grief, privilege, insecurity, addiction, identity, love—anxiety feeds off them all. Anxiety is part of being human. It tells us we're still standing. It tells us we're still alive.

But too much anxiety, like too much of anything, is toxic to our mind, body, and soul.

What is Anxiety?

Definitions of anxiety vary. Anxiety to me is a crawling, ever-circling predator that feeds on fear and devours the things I love. It's an overwhelming feeling of worry and sense of dread that can spiral out of control sometimes. Which is why I put a lot of time and energy into self-care.

Anxiety is the big brother of stress, toxic stress. It's good to know this because, as you'll discover proactively managing your stress levels and engaging in activities that increase resilience can help you tame this bully easily.

Most of us feel worried at some point in our lives and experience situations that can cause us to feel anxious. While the 'right' amount of anxiety can help us perform better and stimulate action, too much anxiety can tip things out of balance.

Feelings of worry or anxiety are part of a healthy emotional experience. Feeling anxious can warn you and urge you to take care. But when it comes to an intense, prolonged experience, anxiety can be excruciating, unbearable and even debilitating.

In the absence of panic attacks, we may think we are just worrying too much. Our struggles of constant worry may be ignored, minimized or dismissed and, in turn, not properly diagnosed, healed or treated. This is also the case for those with undiagnosed trauma.

You may be surprised to learn how dismissing the impact of traumatic events is negatively impacting your anxiety. You may feel as I once did those things that have happened to you are, "normal" and "just a fact of life." You may be heartened to discover that in no way has your life been normal. Sometimes unearthing the truth provides tremendous clarity and healing. It did for me. It will for you.

Actress Glenn Close recently revealed how her childhood gave her 'a kind of Post Traumatic Stress Disorder (PSTD)'. Only in her sixties did she seek help to heal the emotional trauma of being raised within a right-wing religious cult for thirteen years when she was just seven.

"I visited a childhood trauma specialist not too long ago—even at my age which is kind of astounding. But it establishes these trigger points that affect you for the rest of your life," Close revealed in an interview in 2018.

"I think anybody who has gone through any kind of experience like that doesn't want to be affected by it. I think it really is interesting how deep it runs," she said.

Similarly, a client of mine who had suffered childhood sexual abuse as a young boy, waited forty years before seeking therapy. He felt so liberated finally purging those wounds and regaining his life.

Symptoms

Anxiety can quickly spiral out of control and contribute to a range of mental health challenges. The primary source used to classify mental illnesses is provided by the American Psychiatric Association and their Diagnostic and Statistical Manual of Mental Disorders known as the DSM.

Professionals referring to the DSM look for factors like excessive, hindering worry paired with a variety of physical symptoms, then use assessments to make a diagnosis, and rule out other possibilities.

The DSM-5, for example, outlines specific criteria, or symptoms, to help professionals diagnose generalized anxiety disorder (GAD) and, in turn, create a more effective plan of care. While some professionals may prescribe medication, as you'll discover in this book, this is not the only, nor always, effective way to treat anxiety.

When assessing for GAD, clinical professionals are looking for the following:

1. The presence of excessive anxiety and worry about a variety of topics, events, or activities. Worry occurs more often than not for at least 6 months and is clearly excessive.
2. The worry is experienced as very challenging to control. The worry in both adults and children may easily shift from one topic to another.
3. The anxiety and worry are accompanied with at least three of the following physical or cognitive symptoms (In children, only one symptom is necessary for a diagnosis of GAD):

- Edginess or restlessness
- Tiring easily; more fatigued than usual
- Impaired concentration or feeling as though the mind goes blank
- Irritability (which may or may not be observable to others)
- Increased muscle aches or soreness
- Difficulty sleeping (due to trouble falling asleep or staying asleep, restlessness at night, or unsatisfying sleep)

Many people suffering from GAD also experience the following symptoms:

- Sweating
- Nausea
- Diarrhoea

However, diagnosis can be an imperfect science, and other medical conditions, lifestyle choices (including excessive alcohol consumption, cannabis and drug use, and undiagnosed traumas) can also lead to similar symptoms.

Your Anxiety Rescue

If you are struggling with excessive worry, which makes it hard to carry out day-to-day activities and responsibilities or increasingly leads you to feel depressed, some of the solutions that follow may be just the rescue remedy you need.

But like any medicine, you do have to take action.

For example, part of my self-care plan includes many of the things we'll discuss in *Anxiety Rescue,* including regular:

- Massage
- Talk-therapy or counselling
- Time alone
- Prayer
- Meditation
- Low consumption of alcohol
- Defragging from social media regularly
- Journaling

In the next chapter, we'll look at some of the ways anxiety is treated, including the growing discontent with pharmaceutical attempts to 'cure' anxiety versus natural ways to increase serotonin and other feel-good hormones in the body-brain.

2

TREATING ANXIETY

As EDMUND J. Bourne (Ph.D.) writes in the preface to the Third Edition of *The Anxiety & Phobia Workbook,* there have been several noteworthy changes in the treatment of anxiety disorders. A major shift has been "to give prescription medication more preference, especially when anxiety symptoms are in the *moderate* to *severe range*."

Borne attributes this in part with the increased awareness of "the role of heredity and neurobiology in the *causation* of anxiety disorders."

My personal and professional view is that while medication intervention can be extremely helpful for some, it should be used with some degree of caution. Part of that caution involves increasing the awareness of how it may be too readily prescribed without a comprehensive analysis of lifestyle or temporary stressors that may be impacting anxiety levels.

And we'll discuss throughout *Anxiety Rescue, how* in our Western culture, so many people drink excessively, use recreational drugs, over-work, bottle up their feelings, lead sedentary lives, don't switch off, endure toxic and narcissistic relationships, have undiagnosed and untreated trauma—and a vast range of other factors that can lead to excessive worry and anxiety.

Even with the best intentions, a 15-minute doctor's visit will seldom unearth these triggers and certainly won't heal them. Some therapists have suggested it can take up to three months of repeated visits before clients feel comfortable and safe enough to reveal the real sources of their anxiety.

Intimacy takes time. Which explains, in part, why prescription medication has become the drug of choice.

While any approach that relieves suffering should be utilized science has sometimes been at odds with the notion that people can cure themselves.

I'm also increasingly alarmed by the side effects that many of my clients suffer—including depression and suicidal thoughts. Others, just feel tired, lethargic, and demotivated. Some become fat.

In the pages that follow, my intent is to provide ideas, strategies, and suggestions that have been helpful for me personally and for my clients. However, as I'm sure you appreciate they are not intended as a substitute for psychotherapy, counseling, or consulting with your physician.

As a holistic therapist and life coach I know there is a wide range of alternative healing approaches that yield remarkable, extremely quick results. It concerns me, and a lot of other health professionals, that too often people turn to anti-anxiety and antidepressant medication, despite research that cites the lower effectiveness and adverse side-effects.

For many people, this still appears to be the solution of choice prescribed by many medical professions.

"Pills are cheap," my doctor told me when I asked her why counseling and therapy weren't recommended to more people. It may be cheap, but worryingly it is not always effective and the side-effects can also do more harm than healing.

Masking Pain Does Not Offer Long-Term Relief

Rather than offer short-term help very often people come to rely on medical prescriptions for decades. In an extract from his book, <u>Lost Connections: Uncovering The Real Causes of Depression – and the Unexpected Solutions,</u> Johann Hari, who took antidepressants for 13 years, says masking the pain does not offer long-term relief and calls for a new approach.

> "I was a teenager when I swallowed my first antidepressant. I was standing in the weak English sunshine, outside a pharmacy in a shopping centre in London. The tablet was white and small, and as I swallowed, it felt like a chemical kiss," Hari says.
>
> "That morning I had gone to see my doctor and I had told him – crouched, embarrassed – that pain was leaking out of me uncontrollably, like a bad smell, and I had felt this way for several years. In reply, he told me a story.
>
> "'There is a chemical called serotonin that makes people feel good, he said, and some people are naturally lacking it in their brains. You are clearly one of those people. There are now, thankfully, new drugs that will restore your serotonin level to that of a normal person. Take them, and you will be well.'
>
> "At last, I understood what had been happening to me, and why. However, a few months into my drugging,

something odd happened. The pain started to seep through again. Before long, I felt as bad as I had at the start.

"I went back to my doctor, and he told me that I was clearly on too low a dose. And so, 20 milligrams became 30 milligrams; the white pill became blue. I felt better for several months. And then the pain came back through once more. My dose kept being jacked up, until I was on 80mg, where it stayed for many years, with only a few short breaks. And still the pain broke back through."

You can read a summary of Hari's views, including his claims of an over-riding profit motive by pharmaceutical companies, in his interview with The Guardian. 'Is everything you think you know about depression wrong?"

A GOOD THERAPIST will often share strategies that can help you rebalance the hormones in your brain, or refer you to other health professionals like nutritionists and dieticians.

As you'll discover in *Anxiety Rescue*, there are numerous ways to increase serotonin in your brain without drugs: including meditation, exercise, sunlight, vitamins and other low-cost approaches.

Many of these approaches will save you money, boost your health, help you reduce weight and improve your relationships. One of these strategies—eliminating or cutting back alcohol consumption—is one I discuss in the chapter Mindful Drinking.

Alcohol has been found to significantly reduce serotonin 45 minutes after drinking. As this article in Spirit-Science claims, there is also a clear link between alcohol consumption, anger, violence, suicide and other types of aggressive behavior. Aggression is also heavily linked to low serotonin levels and may be due to alcohol's disrupting effects on serotonin metabolism.

In New Zealand, where talk-therapy or counseling was once generously funded by the Government, several years ago this was diverted to the seemingly more (cost) effective method of prescription medicine. Interestingly, in 2019, moves are afoot to rewrite the imbalance and provide more mental health services, including counselling.

As Bourne also notes, "As a counterpoint to prescription medications, there has also been an increased interest in the use of herbs and natural agents to reduce anxiety. I believe these substances can be quite helpful—some more for anxiety, some more for depression—when such problems are in the *mild* to *moderate* range of severity.

Holistic Health

I first met Alice Morris in 1997 when I went in search of something to help alleviate my soaring stress levels. Other recruitment consultants I worked with at the Global Recruitment agency, where I later developed shingles, swore by her holistic healing approach.

Back in the 90s, her approach was innovative—considered almost heretical in the eyes of the mainstream medical profession. Now, much of what she offers, including acupuncture, has been scientifically validated and embraced.

Alice and her multifaceted approach to managing acute anxiety and toxic stress was my first introduction to mind, body, and soul healing.

And it helped. It helped a lot. Especially her massage, acupuncture, and some of the herbs she prescribed for me.

However, as you'll learn in *Anxiety Rescue* unless the root cause is addressed, i.e. my toxic work situation, Alice's approach, as with any other, just helped me tread water for a little longer.

When my nervous system finally yelled, "Pay Attention," and I developed shingles, I knew I could no longer lie to myself. I knew I had to leave my job. I share my exact strategy and more of my story in my *Mid-Life Career Rescue* series of books.

As you'll read from Alice's story, she also left a less than ideal, yet esteemed career, to follow her true calling. I am grateful to Alice—I credit her work with helping me regain control of the reins of my anxiety and to helping me stay alive—restoring me to strength until such time as I could leave.

> "My parents wanted me to be secure in my life in China and their expectations like most Chinese parents were for their children to get a good education and get a high position job so I studied accountancy for 5 years and worked for a big wholesale electrical appliance company as a senior accountant, a job position in which I was the envy of many people at the time.
>
> Even though this was a very successful job and I was considered a success I was not happy in doing it.
>
> In 1990 at the age of 29, I decided to move to New Zealand to follow my dream of understanding true health. This was the perfect opportunity to start doing Chinese medicine again. I worked in Auckland for 4 years doing herbs and acupressure.
>
> In 1995 I set up the Wellington Health Massage Clinic followed by the Alice Qigong and Acupressure school. I also returned to China frequently from 1996

studying in Xanxi ,Fujian, Anhui, Tai Yuan in Qigong, Fung shui, Chinese Astrology and medicine.

In 2007 I completed an advanced two-month course in Beijing on food healing formulas with Professor Liu who has over 270 branches in China and is one of the leading authorities of the ancient Chinese food healing techniques which is having outstanding results in mainland China.

Through this work I found the New Zealand climate and culture was quite different from China so I had to adjust my treatment according to New Zealand conditions and realised that including Herbs, acupressure, and acupuncture is not enough.

I have found peoples health is not just what the traditional healing methods of acupuncture, acupressure and herbs is but far more including their beliefs, what food they eat, their working state, family state, living environment, general health constitution, lifestyle and their time and date of birth (Chinese Astrology).

A holistic approach is a much deeper way of addressing your health."

Throughout *Anxiety Rescue* you'll discover a range of natural antidepressants and anxiety-reducing strategies. Importantly, you'll learn empowering strategies that will help you be less dependent on the drug companies and more in control of you and your life.

My hope is that in the process you will experience a feeling of profound joy and peace—a 'feeling of being at home' and reclaiming what you once felt was lost, broken, or missing from your life.

But first, let's try and pinpoint just what's making you anxious.

3
WHAT MAKES YOU ANXIOUS?

Sometimes when you name the beast you can tame the beast.

Here are just a few of many things that can increase feelings of anxiety:

- Mounting debt
- Job loss
- Burnout and stress
- Relationship issues
- Conflict at work
- Public speaking
- Exams and performance appraisals
- Bullying
- Toxic people
- Narcissism
- Trauma
- Fear

Here are a few other common culprits:

- Career dissatisfaction (the job itself, overwork)
- Colleagues or bosses at work
- Health (depression, self-image, weight, illness, etc.)
- Environmental (noise, weather, chaos, etc.)
- Toxic work environments
- Financial uncertainty
- Values conflicts
- Uncertainty
- Change (keeping up with technology)
- Information obesity/overload
- Bombardment/decision fatigue
- Cumulative stress
- The political climate/leadership fears

Lifestyle and health choices can also increase feelings of anxiety including:

- Alcohol consumption and drug use
- Poor diet
- Vitamin deficiencies
- Lack of exercise
- Technology use, including phone overuse
- Social media
- Lack of, or disrupted, sleep
- Lack of work-life balance

Chemical imbalances in your brain and gut may also be the culprit. Including to much or too little of:

- Serotonin
- Dopamine
- Norepinephrine

- Noradrenaline
- and other chemicals, hormones and neurotransmitters

If you're wondering if the symptoms you're having are caused by a chemical imbalance, it's important to know that there's quite a bit of controversy surrounding this theory.

In fact, it's been largely refuted by the medical community. Researchers argue that the chemical imbalance hypothesis is more of a figure of speech.

It doesn't really capture the true complexity of these disorders. In other words, anxiety and other mental disorders aren't simply caused by chemical imbalances in the brain. As I've already highlighted, there's a lot more complexity to them, and there's also a myriad of natural ways to correct any imbalance.

The chemical imbalance theory also doesn't explain how these chemicals become unbalanced in the first place.

As Harvard Medical School reports, there are likely millions of different chemical reactions occurring in your brain at any given time. These are responsible for your mood and overall feelings. It's impossible to tell if anyone truly has a chemical imbalance in their brain at a given time.

The most common evidence used to support the chemical imbalance theory is the effectiveness of anti-anxiety and anti-depressant medications. These medications work by increasing the amounts of serotonin and other neurotransmitters in the brain.

However, just because your mood can be elevated with drugs that increase brain chemicals doesn't mean that your symptoms were caused by a deficiency in that chemical in the first place. It's just as possible that low serotonin levels are just another symptom of depression, not the cause.

There are no reliable tests to identify imbalances in your brain. Firstly, not all neurotransmitters are produced in the brain. Secondly, neurotransmitter levels in your body and brain are constantly and rapidly changing. This makes tests unreliable.

Thyroid and other disorders can also trigger symptoms of anxiety and other mental disorders.

When it comes to anxiety, there are likely many factors at play. As, you'll discover in the next chapter, even some of the most successful people can suffer from, and recover from, crippling anxiety.

DID YOU ENJOY THIS EXCERPT?

Are you driving through life with the handbrake on? Is anxiety, fear, stress, or depression preventing you from finding happiness and achieving your fullest potential?

Is anxiety preventing you from having the ultimate career, loving relationship, excellent health?

End fear. Stop crippling anxiety and panic attacks now... easily and naturally—medication-free.

"Cassandra's book is for anyone interested in ending anxiety issues, but also, for those who seek deeper meaning in their lives. Anxiety Rescue covers a range of healing methods and a variety of topics, from self-acceptance, to prosperity. It's a book about total well-being. Cassandra restates the wisdom of Leonardo Da Vinci, Coco Chanel and other important historical and modern-day figures who have much to teach about authenticity and success. An uplifting, informative and inspirational work! I highly recommend Anxiety Rescue."

~ **Valeria Teles, author Fit For Joy**

"I was expecting a mental health-type book interlaced with scientific fact but, instead, received an uplifting book with a catalog of ideas, intertwined with the historical endeavors of Leonardo da Vinci and Coco Chanel. Learning about these two people while navigating how to rid my life of anxiety was fun and playful. I'm grateful to the author for taking this approach as I feel like I have a path that can easily be followed now. I highly recommend this book!"

~ **Amazon Review**

"Cassandra explores the nature of anxiety and the effect it has on our physical, emotional, and spiritual self. She draws on much of her research and writings from others of her self-help books. In true Cassandra Gaisford style of practical application - this book is for committed self-helpers."

~ **Catherine Sloan, Counsellor**

ALSO BY THE AUTHOR

Mid-Life Career Rescue:

The Call for Change
What Makes You Happy
Employ Yourself
Job Search Strategies That Work
3 Book Box Set: The Call for Change, What Makes You Happy, Employ Yourself
4 Book Box Set: The Call for Change, What Makes You Happy, Employ Yourself, Job Search Strategies That Work

The Art of Living:

How to Find Your Passion and Purpose
How to Find Your Passion and Purpose Companion Workbook
Career Rescue: The Art and Science of Reinventing Your Career and Life
Boost Your Self-Esteem and Confidence
Anxiety Rescue

Also by the Author

Journaling Prompts Series:

The Passion Journal
The Passion-Driven Business Planning Journal
How to Find Your Passion and Purpose 2 Book-Bundle Box Set

Health & Happiness:

The Happy, Healthy Artist
Stress Less. Love Life More
Bounce: Overcoming Adversity, Building Resilience and Finding Joy
Bounce Companion Workbook

Mindful Sobriety:

Mind Your Drink: The Surprising Joy of Sobriety
Mind Over Mojitos: How Moderating Your Drinking Can Change Your Life:Easy Recipes for Happier Hours & a Joy-Filled Life
Your Beautiful Brain: Control Alcohol and Love Life More

Happy Sobriety:
Happy Sobriety: Non-Alcoholic Guilt-Free Drinks You'll Love
The Sobriety Journal
Happy Sobriety Two Book Bundle-Box Set: Alcohol and Guilt-Free Drinks You'll Love & The Sobriety Journal

Money Manifestation:

Financial Rescue: The Total Money Makeover: Create Wealth, Reduce Debt & Gain Freedom

The Prosperous Author:

Developing a Millionaire Mindset
Productivity Hacks: Do Less & Make More
Two Book Bundle-Box Set (Books 1-2)

Miracle Mindset:

Change Your Mindset: Millionaire Mindset Makeover: The Power of Purpose, Passion, & Perseverance

More of Cassandra's practical and inspiring workbooks on a range of career and life enhancing topics can be found on her website (www.cassandragaisford.com) and her author page at all good online bookstores.

FOLLOW YOUR PASSION TO PROSPERITY ONLINE COURSE

IF YOU NEED MORE HELP to find and live your life purpose you may prefer to take my online course, and watch inspirational and practical videos and other strategies to help you to fulfill your potential.

Follow your passion and purpose to prosperity— online coaching program

Easily discover your passion and purpose, overcoming barriers to success, and create a job or business you love with my self-paced online course.

Gain unlimited lifetime access to this course, for as long as you like—across any and all devices you own. Be supported with practical, inspirational, easy-to-access strategies to achieve your dreams.

To start achieving outstanding personal and professional results with absolute certainty and excitement. **Click here to enroll or find out more— https://the-coaching-lab.teachable.com/p/follow-your-passion-and-purpose-to-prosperity**

FURTHER RESOURCES

Surf The Net

www.bornthisway.foundation
   Founded by Lady Gaga to empower youth, inspire bravery and encourage kindness. Offers inspiration, support, and research to promote mental health.

Mathew Johnstone has a wide range of books and resources on mental wellness and mindfulness: www.matthewjohnstone.com.au

Brad Yates shares a wonderful way to self-help your way through anxiety to self-love in his YouTube videos. You can check it one of them here—https://youtu.be/K6kq9N9Yp6E

www.whatthebleep.com—a powerful and inspiring site emphasizing quantum physics and the transformational power of thought.

www.heartmath.org—comprehensive information and tools help you access your intuitive insight and heart-based knowledge. Validated and supported by science-based research. Check out the additional information about your heart-brain.

Join polymath Tim Ferris and learn from his interesting and informative guests on The Tim Ferris Show http://fourhourworkweek.com/podcast/.

Listen to podcasts which inspire you to become the best version of your writing self—*Joanna Penn's podcast* is very helpful for "authorpreneurs" http://www.thecreativepenn.com/podcasts. I also love Neil Patel's podcast for savvy marketing strategies http://neilpatel.com/podcast.

Experience the transformative power of hypnosis. One of my favorite hypnosis sites is the UK-based Uncommon Knowledge. On their website http://www.hypnosisdownloads.com you'll find a range of self-hypnosis mp3 audios, including The Millionaire Mindset program.

Celebrity hypnotherapist and author Marissa Peer is another favorite source of subconscious reprogramming and liberation—www.marisapeer.com.

What beliefs are holding you back? Check out Peer's Youtube clip "How To Teach Your Mind That Everything Is Available To You" here—https://www.youtube.com/watch?v=IKeaAbM2kJg

Enjoy James Clear's fabulous blog content and receive further self-improvement tips based on proven scientific research: http://jamesclear.com/articles

Tim Ferriss recommends a couple of apps for those wanting some help getting started with meditation—Headspace (www.headspace.com) or Calm (www.calm.com).

National Geographic: The Science of Stress: Portrait of a killer
https://www.youtube.com/watch?v=ZyBsy5SQxqU

Effects of Stress on Your Body
https://www.youtube.com/watch?v=1p6EeYwp1O4

Mindfulness training
Wellington-based Peter Fernando offers an introductory guided meditation which you can take further. He also meets with individuals and groups in Wellington for philosophical talks on mindfulness and Buddhism. Very enjoyable and great for the soul.
http://www.monthofmindfulness.info

Guided meditations
www.calm.com

Free app with guided meditations
http://eocinstitute.org/meditation/emotional-benefits-of-meditation/
Includes a comprehensive list of the benefits of meditation.

Career Guidance Sites:
www.aarp.org/work - information and tools to help you stay current and connected with what's hot and what's not in today's workplace.

www.lifereimagined.org - loads of inspiration and practical tips to help you maximize your interests and expertise, personalized and interactive.

www.whatthebleep.com – a powerful and inspiring site emphasizing quantum physics and the transformational power of thought.

www.personalitytype.com—created by the authors of *Do What You Are: Discover the Perfect Career for You through the Secrets of Personality Type*. This site focuses on expanding your awareness of your own type and that of others—including children and partners. This site also contains many useful links.

Books

Repurpose trauma with Azita Nahai, *Trauma to Dharma: Transform Your Pain into Purpose*

Treatment of Complex Trauma: A Sequenced, Relationship-Based Approach by Christine Courtois and Julian Ford
   Journey Through Trauma: A Trail Guide to the 5-Phase Cycle of Healing Repeated Trauma by Gretchen Schmelzer, PhD

The Complex PTSD Workbook: A Mind-Body Approach to Regaining Emotional Control and Becoming Whole by Arielle Schwartz, PhD

The Body Keeps Score: Brain, Mind, And Body In The Healing Of Trauma by Bessel van der Kolk

Struggling in an extroverted world? Introverts are enjoying a renaissance, fueled in part by Susan Cain's terrific bestseller, *Quiet: The Power of Introverts in a World That Can't Stop Talking.*

Roll up your sleeves and bring out the big guns to win your creative battle with *The War of Art* by Steven Pressfield.

Power up with a new personality—read Breaking the Habit of Being Yourself: How to Lose Your Mind and Create a New One by Dr. Joe Dispenza.

Unleash the power of your mind by reading *You Are the Placebo: Making Your Mind Matter,* by Dr. Joe Dispenza.

Manifest your prosperity with Rhonda Byrne in her popular book, *The Secret.*

Ensure you don't starve by reading Jeff Goins collated wisdom in *Real Artists Don't Starve: Timeless Strategies for Thriving in the New Creative Age.*

Fortify your faith with Julia Cameron's book, *Faith and Will.*

How to Survive and Thrive in Any Life Crisis, Dr. Al Siebert

Thrive: The Third Metric to Redefining Success and Creating a Happier Life, Arianna Huffington

(This book has great content throughout and some excellent resources listed in the back.)

The Power of Now: A Guide to Spiritual Enlightenment, Eckhart Tolle

The Book of Joy, The Dalai Lama and Archbishop Desmond Tutu

The Sleep Revolution: Transforming Your Life One Night at a Time, Arianna Huffington

Quiet the Mind: An Illustrated Guide on How to Meditate, Mathew Johnstone

Comfortable with Uncertainty: 108 Teachings on Cultivating Fearlessness and Compassion, Pema Chodron

Power vs. Force: The Hidden Determinants of Human Behavior, David R. Hawkins

Learn how to live an inspired life with Tarot cards and other oracles. Read Jessa Crispin's book, *The Creative Tarot: A Modern Guide to an Inspired Life.*

Check out all of Collette-Baron-Reid's books, including: *Uncharted: The Journey Through Uncertainty to Infinite Possibility* and *Messages from Spirit: The Extraordinary Power of Oracles, Omens, and Signs.*

BLOSSOM

"Blossom into your dharma, that which you are meant to become. It is the music you are playing out in the world."

~ Pam Gregory

ABOUT THE AUTHOR

Cassandra Gaisford, is a holistic therapist, award-winning artist, and #1 bestselling author. A corporate escapee, she now lives and works from her idyllic lifestyle property overlooking the Bay of Islands in New Zealand.

Cassandra is best known for the passionate call to redefine what it means to be successful in today's world.

She is a well-known expert in the area of success, passion, purpose and transformational business, career and life change, and is regularly sought after as a keynote speaker, and by media seeking an expert opinion on career and personal development issues.

Cassandra has also contributed to international publications and been interviewed on national radio and television in New Zealand and America.

She has a proven-track record of success helping people find savvy ways to boost their finances, change careers, build a business or become a solopreneur—on a shoestring.

Cassandra's unique blend of business experience and qualifications (BCA, Dip Pych.), creative skills, and wellness and holistic training (Dip Counselling, Reiki Master Teacher) blends pragmatism and commercial savvy with rare and unique insight and out-of-the-box-thinking for anyone wanting to achieve an extraordinary life.

Learn more about her on her website, her blog, or connect with her on Facebook and Twitter.

STAY IN TOUCH
FOLLOW ME AND CONTINUE TO BE INSPIRED

Follow Me And Continue To Be Supported, Encouraged, and Inspired

www.cassandragaisford.com
www.facebook.com/cassandra.gaisford
www.instagram.com/cassandragaisford
www.youtube.com/cassandragaisfordnz
www.pinterest.com/cassandraNZ
www.linkedin.com/in/cassandragaisford
www.twitter.com/cassandraNZ

BLOG

Be inspired by regular posts to help you increase your wellness, follow your bliss, slay self-doubt, and sustain healthy habits.

Learn more about how to achieve happiness and success at work and life by visiting my blog:

www.cassandragaisford.com/archives

SPEAKING EVENTS

Cassandra is available internationally for speaking events aimed at wellness strategies, motivation, inspiration and as a keynote speaker.

She has an enthusiastic, humorous and passionate style of delivery and is celebrated for her ability to motivate, inspire and enlighten.

For information navigate to www.cassandragaisford.com/contact/speaking

To ask Cassandra to come and speak at your workplace or conference, contact: cassandra@cassandragaisford.com

NEWSLETTERS

For inspiring tools and helpful tips subscribe to Cassandra's free newsletters here:
http://www.cassandragaisford.com

Sign up now and receive a free eBook to help you find your passion and purpose!

http://eepurl.com/bEArfT

ABOUT THE AUTHOR

CASSANDRA GAISFORD is best known as *The Queen of Uplifting Inspiration*.

A former holistic therapist, award-winning artist, and #1 bestselling author. A corporate escapee, she now lives and works from her idyllic lifestyle property overlooking the Bay of Islands in New Zealand.

Cassandra's unique blend of business experience and qualifications (BCA, Dip Psych.), creative skills, and wellness and holistic training (Dip Counselling, Reiki Master Teacher) blends pragmatism and commercial savvy with rare and unique insight and out-of-the-box-thinking for anyone wanting to achieve an extraordinary life.

ALSO BY CASSANDRA GAISFORD

Transformational Super Kids:

The Little Princess
The Little Princess Can Fly
I Have to Grow
The Boy Who Cried
Jojo Lost Her Confidence
Lulu is a Black Sheep

Mid-Life Career Rescue:

The Call for Change
What Makes You Happy
Employ Yourself
Job Search Strategies That Work
3 Book Box Set: The Call for Change, What Makes You Happy, Employ Yourself
4 Book Box Set: The Call for Change, What Makes You Happy, Employ Yourself, Job Search Strategies That Work

Also by Cassandra Gaisford

Career Change:

Career Change 2020 5 Book-Bundle Box Set

Master Life Coach:

Leonardo da Vinci: Life Coach
Coco Chanel: Life Coach

The Art of Living:

How to Find Your Passion and Purpose
How to Find Your Passion and Purpose Companion Workbook
Career Rescue: The Art and Science of Reinventing Your Career and Life
Boost Your Self-Esteem and Confidence
Anxiety Rescue
No! Why 'No' is the New 'Yes'
How to Find Your Joy and Purpose
How to Find Your Joy and Purpose Companion Workbook

The Art of Success:

Leonardo da Vinci
Coco Chanel

Journaling Prompts Series:

The Passion Journal
The Passion-Driven Business Planning Journal
How to Find Your Passion and Purpose 2 Book-Bundle Box Set

Health & Happiness:

The Happy, Healthy Artist
Stress Less. Love Life More
Bounce: Overcoming Adversity, Building Resilience and Finding Joy
Bounce Companion Workbook

Mindful Sobriety:

Mind Your Drink: The Surprising Joy of Sobriety
Mind Over Mojitos: How Moderating Your Drinking Can Change Your Life: Easy Recipes for Happier Hours & a Joy-Filled Life
Your Beautiful Brain: Control Alcohol and Love Life More

Happy Sobriety:

Happy Sobriety: Non-Alcoholic Guilt-Free Drinks You'll Love
The Sobriety Journal
Happy Sobriety Two Book Bundle-Box Set: Alcohol and Guilt-Free Drinks You'll Love & The Sobriety Journal

Money Manifestation:

Financial Rescue: The Total Money Makeover: Create Wealth, Reduce Debt & Gain Freedom

The Prosperous Author:

Developing a Millionaire Mindset
Productivity Hacks: Do Less & Make More

Two Book Bundle-Box Set (Books 1-2)

Miracle Mindset:

Change Your Mindset: Millionaire Mindset Makeover: The Power of Purpose, Passion, & Perseverance

Non-Fiction:

Where is Salvator Mundi?

More of Cassandra's practical and inspiring workbooks on a range of career and life-enhancing topics are on her website (www.cassandragaisford.com) and her author page at all good online bookstores.

NOW IN AUDIO!

Did you know you can enjoy and be inspired by Cassandra's most popular and successful books on audio? In less than 15 minutes you could be listening your way to a new life!

Check out the following written and narrated by Cassandra:

Mid-Life Career Rescue: The Career For Change
How to Find Your Passion and Purpose
How to Find Your Joy and Purpose
The Little Princess
The Little Princess Can Fly
I Have to Grow
The Boy Who Cried

Audio versions of these and other titles available now from all online bookstores and libraries.

NEW RELEASES

Word By Word:Lessons on Writing, Love, and Life
Think Outside The Box: How to Change Careers with Creative Thinking

PLEASE LEAVE A REVIEW

Word of mouth is the most powerful marketing force in the universe. If you found this book useful, I'd appreciate you rating this book and leaving a review. You don't have to say much—just a few words about how the book helped you learn something new or made you feel.

"Your books are a fantastic resource and until now I never even thought to write a review. Going forward I will be reviewing more books. So many great ones out there and I want to support the amazing people that write them."
Great reviews help people find good books.

Thank you so much! I appreciate you!

PS: If you enjoyed this book, do me a small favour to help spread the word about it and share on Facebook, Twitter and other social networks.

STAY IN TOUCH

Become a fan and Continue To Be Supported, Encouraged, and Inspired

Subscribe to my newsletter and follow me on BookBub (https://www.bookbub.com/profile/cassandra-gaisford) and be the first to know about my new releases and giveaways

www.cassandragaisford.com
www.facebook.com/powerfulcreativity
www.instagram.com/cassandragaisford
www.youtube.com/cassandragaisfordnz
www.pinterest.com/cassandraNZ
www.linkedin.com/in/cassandragaisford
www.twitter.com/cassandraNZ

And please, do check out some of my videos where I share strategies and tips to stress less and love life more—http://www.youtube.com/cassandragaisfordnz

BLOG

Subscribe and be inspired by regular posts to help you increase your wellness, follow your bliss, slay self-doubt, and sustain healthy habits.

Learn more about how to achieve happiness and success at work and life by visiting my blog:

www.cassandragaisford.com/archives

SPEAKING EVENTS

Cassandra is available internationally for speaking events aimed at wellness strategies, motivation, inspiration and as a keynote speaker.

She has an enthusiastic, humorous and passionate style of delivery and is celebrated for her ability to motivate, inspire and enlighten.

For information navigate to www.cassandragaisford.com/contact/speaking

To ask Cassandra to come and speak at your workplace or conference, contact: cassandra@cassandragaisford.com

NEWSLETTERS

For inspiring tools and helpful tips subscribe to Cassandra's free newsletters here:
http://www.cassandragaisford.com

Sign up now and receive a free eBook to help you find your passion and purpose!
http://eepurl.com/bEArfT

COPYRIGHT

Copyright © 2019, 2020 Cassandra Gaisford
Published by Blue Giraffe Publishing 2019, 2020

Blue Giraffe Publishing is a division of Worklife Solutions Ltd.

Cover Design by Cassandra Gaisford

All rights reserved. No part of this publication may be reproduced, distributed, or transmitted in any form or by any means, including photocopying, recording, or other electronic or mechanical methods, without the prior written permission of the author or publisher, except in the case of brief quotations embodied in reviews and certain other non-commercial uses permitted by copyright law.

Neither the publisher nor the author are engaged in rendering professional advice or services to the individual reader. The ideas, procedures, and suggestions contained in this book are not intended as a substitute for psychotherapy, counselling, or consulting with your physician.

The intent of the author is only to offer information of a general nature to help you in your quest for emotional, physical, and spiritual well-being.

Any use of information in this book is at the reader's discretion and risk. Neither the author nor the publisher can be held responsible for any loss, claim or damage arising out of the use, or misuse, of the suggestions made, the failure to take medical advice or for any material on third party websites.

ISBN PRINT: 978-0-9951138-0-0
ISBN EBOOK: 978-0-9951137-9-4

First Edition

www.ingramcontent.com/pod-product-compliance
Lightning Source LLC
Chambersburg PA
CBHW020255030426
42336CB00010B/778